100 Ways to Become a Better, Smarter, Prouder, Stronger, and More Respected Leader

The Courageous Leader's Pocket Companion

by Martina Sprague

Copyright 2012 Martina Sprague

All rights reserved. No part of this book may be reproduced in any form or by any means, electronic or otherwise, without the prior written consent of the author.

Front cover photo: Martina Sprague

Image source for horse logo (slightly adapted) on back cover: CoralieM Photographie, Wikimedia Commons.

"Consider with thyself what thou art man enough to undertake . . . for to take up great resolutions, and then to lay them aside, would only end in dishonor."

--Snorri Sturluson, from King Olaf Trygvason's Saga, Heimskringla: The Chronicle of the Kings of Norway

TABLE OF CONTENTS

Introduction	10
Accepting Your Findings	13
Acting on the Obvious	14
Agreeing on the Premises	15
Aid to Judgment	16
Another's Greatness	18
Applying Pressure	19
Ask the Team	20
Average Is a Copout	21
Better to Be Healthy and Rich	22
Broken Spirit	23
Building-Blocks of Teams	24
Byproduct of a Well-Run Team	25
Calling a Spade a Spade	26
Can You Hear the Talk?	27
Catch-22	28
Causing Friction	29

Charging the Air	30
Cheese, Fish, and Carrots	31
Cherry-Picking for Evidence	32
Choosing Your Lens	34
Correspondence Principle	35
Cosmic Clause	36
Critique versus Criticism	37
Cut and Run	38
Do You Have Any Questions?	39
Dumb Questions and Dumb People	41
Efficiency versus Energy	42
Eight Hours of Work and a Paycheck	43
Elastic Limit	44
Empty Suit	45
End versus Means	46
Everybody = Nobody	47
Facts and Hypotheses	48
Feed the Team First	50
Feeling Cool	51

Flag to Die For	52
Four-Letter Words	53
Freeing Your Mind of Clutter	54
Gone Fishin'	55
Hearts and Minds	56
History Lesson	57
If a Tree Falls in the Forest	59
"I" In Team	60
Intellectual Growth	61
In the Eye of the Beholder	62
In the Fishbowl	63
In the Trenches	64
I Own, You Own	65
Issues of Passion	66
It's Raining	67
Just a Number	68
Know Where You Are Going	69
Lesson in Logic and Truth	70
Liking Things the Way They Are	71

Limited Scope of the Mind	72
Made Or Born?	73
Matter of Timing	74
Moral Courage	75
Mutual Exclusivity	76
Nothing to Complain About	77
Number 10 and Why Size Matters	78
Oh, Did I Tell You I Took Second Place?	79
Open versus Closed Doors	80
Optimized Team	81
Organizing Your Thoughts	82
Payoff	84
Preserving the Hunger	85
Proper Thinking	86
Proverbial Shit	87
Ready to Peak	88
Reality versus Passion	89
Resistance to Change	90
Reward and Punishment	92

Right from the Beginning	93
Room for Improvement?	94
Scientific Method	96
Sitting on Two Chairs	97
Situational Awareness	98
Size versus Strength	99
Smarter, Not Harder	100
Spotting a Leader	101
Steppingstones	102
Strategy and Tactics	104
Tangible Returns	105
Team Discrimination	106
Therefore I Am	107
Thinking the Thought to Conclusion	108
To Hell and Back	109
Top of the Mountain	110
Transmitting the Message	111
Truth versus Rumor	112
Very Does Not Make It More So	113

What *Can* You Do?	114
What Is, What Could Have Been	115
What, Where, How, and Why	116
When Preparation and Opportunity Meet	117
Which Way Is the Wheel Turning?	118
Who Wants a Challenge?	119
Winning Matters	120
World's Greatest	121
Conclusion	122

INTRODUCTION

Who becomes a leader? The leader is set apart from the rest; you are in your position because you have worked hard and are committed, and because you have certain qualities that prove helpful to the workers and the company. At least this is the way it is supposed to be. But in reality people choose their leader regardless of his or her title. You don't become a leader by placing a "supervisor" patch on your shirt; you become a leader by exercising a set of qualities that make others want to follow.

When you become a leader, you also embrace the responsibility that comes with your title. Because of your position, people will look up to you and ask your advice. They expect you to know a little more than they do; they expect you to be trustworthy and helpful. If you play your cards right, you can have a drastic effect on the people you lead. And when you affect this base positively, it will become stable and energetic and ready to lift your company into world class status. When you step past what you thought possible, when you succeed at motivating others, they will look forward to coming to work. And when leaving at the day's end, they will feel energized and look forward to coming back tomorrow.

This book is an easy reference that the leader can use every day to seek inspiration on a number of topics, including leader integrity, communication, establishing and maintaining vision, creating a winning team, delegation of duties, and critique and evaluation. The suggestions are arranged alphabetically and not in any particular order of importance.

The author firmly believes that any leadership model requires an intellectual pursuit that exceeds the "cookbook for success" approach. This book admittedly expresses much in a few words and therefore requires considerable thought and self-reflection, which may leave the reader curious and in search of more detailed information. To learn about the reasoning behind the suggestions, and how and why the author reached the conclusions she did, she recommends that the reader picks up a copy of *Leadership, It Ain't Rocket Science: A Critical Analysis of Moving With the Cheese and Other Motivational Leadership Bullshit*, which is a serious and in-depth study of leadership from an analytical rather than motivational angle, and is meant to stir at least some controversy and incite the reader to throw off the yoke of ambiguity when attempting to establish a leadership approach that works with his or her team.

"Character is simply habit long continued."

--Pliny the Younger (c. 62-112 CE), Roman writer and governor

ACCEPTING YOUR FINDINGS

If you implement plans and procedures without truly understanding the underlying reasons, you will lose the trust of your team, be predestined for failure, and later try to save face when your team has thrashed you.

1. Asking pertinent questions is a prerequisite for gaining insight into leadership.

2. Those who fail to ask questions cannot lead others, because even if they know where they want to go, they will not know how to get there, what happens if they take the wrong fork in the road, or how to correct problems.

3. When analyzing a problem, learn to distinguish between what you see and what you wish to see. Be ready to accept your findings even if they are not what you wish them to be.

TIP: Never say "no thanks" to information. Accept what is handed to you, and decide later which parts you will take to heart and which you will discard.

ACTING ON THE OBVIOUS

The difficulty lies not in stating the obvious but in bringing the obvious to action.

1. When the outcome of an act conforms to predictions, it is easy to fall into the trap of believing that the principle used to achieve success will hold true in all situations.

2. The analytically driven leader will examine also those cases where the particular principle failed to achieve success.

3. The checklist approach (or cookbook for success often promoted as a quick and easy way to be a good leader) reduces a profoundly human activity such as leadership to a science, and provides a means for avoiding critical thinking.

TIP: Good leaders need broad horizons, which is all the more reason to develop critical thinking skills, discuss unpleasant facts, and avoid falling in lockstep with the many popular slogans that are so frequently recited in books and at leadership seminars.

AGREEING ON THE PREMISES

The danger with taking a scientific approach to leadership is that the use of scientific principles presupposes a leadership style that is based on specific techniques and thus remains unaltered by innovation.

1. The fundamental principle of logic states that if the premises (the examples that set it up) are true, the conclusion will automatically follow.

2. But if the given information (the premises) is incorrect or misleading, setting up an equation for leadership and following it blindly, because "science says it is supposed to work," predestines one for failure.

3. When setting up examples in logic argumentation for the purpose of leadership, *even if* the premises are true the conclusion may NOT automatically follow.

TIP: Before accepting the science, make an effort to determine the validity of the premises and weed out any information that is insufficient or irrelevant.

AID TO JUDGEMENT

If employees take no interest in the affairs of the company for which they work, they become useless (or nearly so) to the company. Debate and discussion are not stumbling-blocks in the way of action, but crucial necessities to wise action.

1. Good leaders understand human nature and avoids going against the grain.

2. Good leaders question, experiment, and research before asking their team to change. They have vision and can look beyond the moment.

3. Talented leaders can hope for a strong position only when their character and familiarity with leadership fortify each other, and only when they obey their own principles which result from their own judgment. But they cannot expect a subordinate to embrace those same principles, unless the subordinate has come to his or her own conclusion that the principles are sound.

TIP: When pursuing leadership in earnest, you will be wise to avoid trampling the path prescribed by well-meaning but gung-ho men and women who spend their days dreaming up all sorts of bumper sticker slogans, which, although possibly proving motivational for a day, lack substance in the real world. Theory should aid judgment but not tell you what to do.

"For one swallow does not make a summer, nor does one fine day; and so too one day, or a short time, does not make a man blessed and happy."

--Aristotle (384-322 BCE), Greek critic and philosopher

ANOTHER'S GREATNESS

If you feel as though you have been in the same ol' grind for twenty years, you probably have.

1. Goals must have duration and you must feel their impact every day.

2. Once the goals have been set, the vision must remain in view. Few people will find meaning in the journey alone without the promise or hope for something "better."

3. If the vision is not desirable, it will have little value. You must have ownership of the vision; you must have reasonable control of the journey. The team must be updated on its progress regularly.

TIP: When you have defined the vision in concrete terms, continue by identifying the obstacles. Remember that much of your motivation stems from the competition: Another's greatness can serve as a catalyst for your own.

APPLYING PRESSURE

Pressure is the ratio of force to the area over which the force is distributed.

1. You must have a fine sense of how much pressure your team can handle before it stops functioning properly.

2. You must similarly decide how to distribute the pressure so that it does not fall on just a few members of the team.

3. How do you find the correct balance between the gung-ho leader (or team) and the pacifist who does not seem to care much one way or the other?

TIP: To keep a constant flow of energy, you must consistently apply pressure, but not so much that it breaks the bonds between team members and destroys unity.

ASK THE TEAM

How do you know that you are a team leader? Is it because it is in your job description? Is it because of that convincing little speech you held during your team leader interview? Is it because you have an outgoing personality and work well with others?

1. The leader is set apart from the rest; he is in his position because he has worked hard and is committed, and because he has certain qualities that will be helpful to the workers and the company.

2. You do not become a leader by placing a "supervisor" patch on your shirt; you become a leader by exercising certain qualities that make others want to follow.

3. Telling somebody what to do is easy; telling them how to do it is more difficult. Writing a long list of desired leadership qualities is easy; defining how it should be done is more difficult.

TIP: What makes your team tick? Do your subordinates see you as a leader? If in doubt, the simplest way to find out is by asking them.

AVERAGE IS A COPOUT

If a critique does not serve the intended purpose—to profit the person receiving the critique—it has failed. The individual critiqued must know how to capitalize on the issues covered in the critique.

1. In addition to identifying strengths and weaknesses, you must provide a satisfactory explanation of how you reached your assessment. When identifying weaknesses, you must provide a specific way to overcome them.

2. Disciplinary action, like critique, is useless unless it leads you a step closer to your objective. If you need to discipline a worker, how can you ensure that the discipline is constructive and more than a way to vent your feelings?

3. Choosing the average score is a copout, because you are in fact saying that you are not completely happy with the employee, but you are not unhappy either. In other words, you can get by with the status quo, which means that there is really no motivation to improve. So what do we do? We get by.

TIP: When evaluating or rating an employee, if you cannot offer specific input, it may be tempting to use an "average" rating. Try to avoid this temptation. Do not rate on a scale from one to five, because it would tempt you to choose "three."

BETTER TO BE HEALTHY AND RICH

It is better to be healthy and rich than sick and poor. But if you are sick and poor, it is better to acknowledge that you are sick and poor than pretend otherwise and fail to strive for a better future.

1. To speak the truth, we need to see things as they are. Assigning a higher meaning to a word does not make it so. Using "displaced" rather than "bumped" does not make it hurt less when you lose your job.

2. Just as we must satisfy our basic needs for food and shelter before we can satisfy our need for self-actualization, we must provide a solid base in the work environment before we can expect better performance.

3. Before you can ask people to give, you must provide them with what they need: equipment, praise, opportunity, someone who cares. Once an individual has these commodities, he or she will be more receptive to working hard and providing great customer service.

TIP: Once motivation is achieved, it needs reinforcement and approval. Build enthusiasm by helping the individual perform successfully in front of his or her peers.

BROKEN SPIRIT

Temporarily winning a heart through a clever slogan or a gung-ho speech is easy, but a broken spirit is difficult to heal.

1. Human relationships such as those that exist in the workplace deal heavily in emotions such as love, joy, fear, anger, and frustration.

2. Emotions determine attitudes. You can therefore not approach human emotions like you do a mathematical equation.

3. Even when a good plan has been carefully crafted and defined and leads to its logical conclusion, a leader who fails to cater to human emotions will likely alienate the team.

TIP: When a seemingly good plan conflicts with employee emotions, listen to your gut and rely on common sense.

BUILDING-BLOCKS OF TEAMS

The company where you work may be a unit outwardly. You know it because of the company colors and widgets on the equipment and worker uniforms. You know it because of the slogans. Yet a functional team must be both varied and strong.

1. The team must function as a unit; this is part of the meaning of no "I" in team.

2. To function as unit, all its parts must be so interrelated that it looks like one. But its strength lies not in the similarities of the many parts that make it up, but in the *differences*.

3. Take a jigsaw puzzle. When completed, it forms a perfect picture, yet no two parts look the same. Each team member holds an intricate piece of the puzzle. If you were building a brick wall you would stagger the bricks for strength.

TIP: Your job as a team leader is not to promote a team that is uniform, but to build a team with complementary qualities. Individuals are the building-blocks of teams.

BYPRODUCT OF A WELL-RUN TEAM

Your team (if it is well-run and efficient) does NOT work for the team leader, the company, or the customer. The team is serving itself. Customer service is a byproduct of a well-run team.

1. The team leader is serving the team. He or she is not serving the customer, the company, or the manager. He is serving the team.

2. The team leader does not wear many hats, as some would have us believe. The team leader has only one responsibility: the team.

3. If you say that you are working for the company, the team, management, your paycheck, and the customer, it would be a cosmic clause statement that dilutes the role of the leader and indicates that you do not have a clear understanding of what it means to be a team leader.

TIP: An outstanding leader must do more for the team than what is naturally expected of him.

CALLING A SPADE A SPADE

Why must every worker have a goal?

1. Some people work for you only because they need to put food on the table and not because they feel any particular allegiance to your company.

2. If we force people to set goals, many employees will set goals that they have not thought much about rather than goals that lead to something of true value.

3. To gain proper understanding you must sometimes be prepared to take the opposite stand and have the moral courage NOT to be politically correct; in fact, the courage to dissent openly.

TIP: If you have a problem with the current accomplishments of your team, it is better to say so straight out and talk about what can be done (in other words, to call a spade a spade), rather than beating around the bush with sublime messages that act as turnoffs to the greater part of the workforce.

CAN YOU HEAR THE TALK?

Conflicts are not necessarily bad, but become so when you fail to understand the essential issue. When a conflict is handled appropriately, it will increase your confidence and deepen your thinking.

1. Do you listen to everybody on your team or just to the people you particularly like; to those who squeal the loudest; or to those who make an effort to seek you out?

2. Do you ask your employees to clarify questions that you don't understand fully? If you don't know the correct answer, do you make an effort to find it?

3. Do you let others finish speaking without interrupting, or do you "put words in their mouth"? If somebody is upset, they might just have a need to vent, and not a need to argue.

4. Are you honest and able to present and accept the facts, or do you push others to accept your values? Give an example.

5. Do you say a definite yes or no when you mean to say a definite yes or no? Do you make your actions match your words?

TIP: Sending mixed messages is detrimental to effective communication. Think about what you want to say before you say it, so that you can say exactly what you want to say. Then make your actions match your words.

CATCH-22

Things can look great in theory or on the drawing board, but when you enter the trenches, events will not come down exactly the way you thought.

1. The Catch-22 is that to get anything done you must go through the chain of command, because only the top has the authority to do something. But the closer you are to the bottom, the less important the matter will seem to the top. Those who can do something about the matter have the least interest in doing anything. But to get anything done, you must enlist the people who are the least interested in doing something.

2. Going through the chain of command is often a terrible sacrifice of time and effort. Your needs will likely get lost in the bureaucracy.

3. A chain tends to break at its weakest link. If the chain breaks, you will get no further than to the broken link.

TIP: Some leeway with principles will always work to your benefit. Managers who try to lead employees from behind a desk in an office located at headquarters many miles away will make faulty assumptions. It is better to skip the chain if you can.

CAUSING FRICTION

Friction is a force resisting motion. It takes energy to overcome friction.

1. When implementing a change that your employees resist, to overcome friction you must first apply a force that is equal to the force of friction just to reach neutral ground.

2. You must then apply an additional force to get the employees moving in the new direction.

3. Change can therefore be tremendously energy consuming and troublesome. If possible, start negotiations for change from a position of minimal friction between your views and those of the employees.

TIP: Evaluate beforehand how much friction the change in a procedure is likely to cause among the employees, and whether or not it will be worth the effort.

CHARGING THE AIR

A chain reaction can provide a great effect through little energy.

1. Negative information can be intensified through a chain reaction.

2. If you are not careful, negative information can have undesirable consequences that will spiral out of control.

3. You can feel the effects of another person's mood or behavior, even if he or she is not directing the behavior toward you in particular. Rather, the atmosphere around this person gets "charged," either positively or negatively.

TIP: Before starting an action (a change in policy, for example), look at the possible consequences and the probability that the action will turn into a chain reaction.

CHEESE, FISH, AND CARROTS

A successful change in attitude must be accompanied by clearly defined real change.

1. A person's attitude toward work is largely driven by internal ambitions, and carrot type motivators work only in limited circumstances (as do fish markets or moving with the cheese, for that matter).

2. People are far more likely to change their attitude about a project if they have some ownership of the idea.

3. Some factors are particularly important in determining how happy we are at work, including permission to decide the specific methods by which we do our job or complete a task.

TIP: A way to test if your ideas have value is to restate them from the perspective of the employees. Is it possible that you believe your team feels ownership of an idea, but when you ask them about it they won't know what you are talking about?

CHERRY-PICKING FOR EVIDENCE

Successful leadership is not a hard science like physics or mathematics, but requires a great deal of individual judgment.

1. A good way to remain objective and avoid getting carried away by your passions, is by restating the opposition's viewpoint from *their* perspective as a check and balance on your own view.

2. Or add a third point of view: How would a bystander, either somebody totally unrelated to the situation or a customer, view the issue if he or she were allowed to observe and offer an opinion?

3. Good leaders deal with what has happened in the past, but avoid making predictions or prescribing future behavior.

TIP: A good leader does not push an ideology. Rather, he or she forms a thesis and examines the issues. If the evidence reveals that the thesis will not work, the leader changes the thesis rather than cherry-picks for evidence that supports the initial idea.

"I have taken all knowledge to be my province."

--Sir Francis Bacon (1561-1626 CE), English statesman and philosopher

CHOOSING YOUR LENS

To get a true image, objects must be viewed from a true position.

1. If you view your team's performance from the outside but don't really experience it firsthand, your opinion of what is happening may be invalid simply because of your position.

2. Depending on where you stand, your frame of reference will differ from somebody else's.

3. A team leader or manager may not see what the employees see, because he or she is literally not in the fray on a daily basis and may therefore make false assumptions about the work environment.

TIP: If you want a clear and truthful view of your policies, you must involve others and ask for their views (you must look at the situation through different lenses), because your view alone may be distorted by a number of factors.

CORRESPONDENCE PRINCIPLE

For a new theory to be valid it must account for the verified results of the old theory; it must *correspond* with the old theory. When evaluating Joe or Jane:

1. Have the results of the old evaluation been fully verified? How?

2. What criteria did the last person evaluating Joe or Jane use? If the criteria have changed or are subjective, will the old evaluation still be valid? An evaluation that is invalid fails to accomplish its intent and is a waste of time.

3. If the old and the new evaluations fail to correspond in the region where the results from the old evaluation have been fully verified, the new evaluation is invalid.

TIP: If a new theory builds on an old theory, accept the new theory first after verifying the validity of the old theory.

COSMIC CLAUSE

A cosmic clause is a statement that is absolute or all encompassing in time and space; for example, the greatest, the world champion, the unbeatable, always, never, for time and eternity, throughout the universe. A cosmic clause description for a leadership book might state:

1. Equally good for leaders and followers of any company throughout the world.

2. Infinitely valuable for professional leaders, the up-and-coming, teams and employees, and the everyday person alike.

3. Everything you ever needed to know and everything you ever will need to know about leadership in any situation.

TIP: A cosmic clause vision dilutes the meaning and importance of the vision. The vision must appeal to somebody in particular—not to everybody. Identify the primary person or group of people you want your vision to influence.

CRITIQUE VERSUS CRITICISM

A critique is "a critical and unbiased analysis," which is not the same as *criticism*.

1. Critique increases motivation, *but only* if the critique is fair and the person critiqued understands its value.

2. Although critique may be unpleasant and invite the possibility of an attack on your person, it doesn't *have* to be unpleasant. When allowed to critique widely we eliminate much subjective thought.

3. For a critique to be valid it must account for the verified results of a former critique.

TIP: When critiquing an employee's performance, for the critique to have meaning you must first ensure that the employee welcomes your input and is in a position to receive it.

CUT AND RUN

Might there be times when it is prudent to cut your losses and run, to abandon the vision or objective for the sake of saving the company or the team? Or is it true that reaching the objective is not about feeling good but about getting it done?

1. If you ask "why" and "what next" before you get there, much of your journey will already be staked out.

2. Asking "why" and "what next" will help clarify if achieving the goal will cost you more than you are willing to pay, and if the achievement will be as valuable as you thought. It might make you open toward considering other more profitable alternatives.

3. When taking the first step, as Prussian military strategist Carl von Clausewitz said, also think about what might be the last.

TIP: When setting goals or stating your vision, try to see what is beyond it. Your vision should not be the end result; it should be a steppingstone toward higher ground.

DO YOU HAVE ANY QUESTIONS?

When communicating, ask questions to draw information, not to test an employee's knowledge. Avoid questions that:

1. Are open-ended: "Do you have any questions?" The answer to an open-ended question is not likely to give you much new insight. It is simply too easy for the employee to say "no."

2. Are complex, require the person to solve a puzzle, or have a catch. This is not a test of who is smarter. The purpose of asking questions is to gain information, and not to quiz the employee on his or her knowledge.

3. Cover everything: "What would you do to increase customer service?" It is better to ask a question that pertains to a particular situation: "When Mrs. Smith complained about the extra fee, name one thing you could have done differently."

4. Give you a choice of this or that: "Should you greet the customer by first name or last name?" These questions are invalid because they force the person to make a choice even if both options are incorrect (or correct for that matter).

5. Lead the employee to always answer "yes." For example: "Do you want a career that rewards you for your achievements?" Or, "Do you want to make six figures a year?" Well, duh, who wouldn't?

TIP: To avoid confusion, make questions concise and ask only one thing at a time. Be sensible but also require that others give you a chance.

"What is great in man is that he is a bridge and not a goal."

--Friedrich Nietzsche (1844-1900 CE), German philosopher

DUMB QUESTIONS AND DUMB PEOPLE

Answering questions may seem easy, particularly if you know the answer, but there is in fact an art involved.

1. Avoid a mechanical answer and make sure you fully understand what is being asked. If in doubt, answer the question by asking another question along the same lines. This may lead to the individual asking the question to answering his or her own question.

2. Look for a response when you have answered the question. If the individual asking the question seems confused, quiet, or indifferent, you might need to elaborate on your answer.

3. When an individual confronts you with a problem, ask *why* in order to trigger his or her thinking process. He will then likely come up with the solution himself. When we derive a solution through our own thinking, we will remember it better and give it greater approval.

4. Avoid yes or no answers. By giving a more thorough answer, you ensure that you really answered what was being asked.

5. It has been said that there are no dumb questions . . . only dumb people. Well, there are in fact both dumb questions and dumb people. But when somebody asks a dumb question, don't ridicule him or her or tell him it's a "no-brainer." The purpose is to gain information not to test another person's intelligence.

TIP: When you sense that an individual is afraid to ask but burns with a desire to know, be generous and take the first step by suggesting an answer or solution.

EFFICIENCY VERSUS ENERGY

How **efficient** something is can be expressed by the ratio of work done over energy used.

1. If you are very efficient, you can do a lot of work without expending a lot of energy. If you expend a lot of energy, you ought to rethink how you do the work.

2. When there is inefficiency much energy is wasted. Work that does not lead to results is a waste of energy

3. What is popularly referred to as "busy work," is work delegated to employees when management does not like them sitting idle.

TIP: Busy work does not make a company more efficient. Busy work and inefficiency in general also tend to have a negative effect on employee pride and motivation and destroy the team's momentum.

EIGHT HOURS OF WORK AND A PAYCHECK

Rewards must be large enough to make a difference. They must be fair.

1. A year-end bonus that is only given to those who have worked for the company at least ten years, will create negative attitudes for those who worked just as hard in the last year but only have one year of service with the company.

2. Most people are not lazy and do not inherently dislike work. But just as a successful marriage requires constant reinforcement, so does a successful team leader/team relationship require constant reinforcement.

3. The leader must be passionate and committed to his or her cause if he is to inspire others to follow. But a speech, although it might demonstrate passion, does not necessarily demonstrate a commitment to reward employees for their efforts.

TIP: Ask yourself what you owe your team and what your team owes you outside of what is stated in your written contract. Or do you owe each other nothing but eight hours of work and a paycheck?

ELASTIC LIMIT

In teamwork elasticity can be related to flexibility.

1. How many times have you heard that you must be flexible and bend with the forces if you want to succeed?

2. The question of importance is how far a material can be stretched without permanent distortion.

3. How far can a team be stretched or asked to change before losing motivation and refusing to spring back to its optimum shape?

TIP: The **elastic limit** is the distance beyond which permanent distortion occurs. In team leadership, you must have a good sense of the location of this limit or breaking point.

EMPTY SUIT

When the company or team experience problems, or when tough times strike, it is better to admit it than pretend otherwise when everybody knows that you are just an "empty suit."

1. First impressions are powerful motivators. But what looks good from afar must also look good from up close.

2. Rewards, like punishment, must be swift and certain in order to have meaning. Rewards must be real (tangible) and significant enough to make a difference.

3. For the team to do great work, the work must matter, the results must matter, and they must matter in the near future.

TIP: When you sense that you are losing the team, stop for a moment and remember that this is their career, too. Don't be an empty suit by making things look good from the outside, while allowing them to rot on the inside.

END VERSUS MEANS

The end is more important than the means, because the means must always be judged in relation to the end they serve. If the end is not achieved, the procedure of going through an evaluation process, for example, is useless.

1. Before implementing a quality assurance program you must first define the end objective: What are you trying to achieve?

2. If you are trying to achieve better workers (whatever that means) but the evaluation serves to antagonize the workers, you have not achieved the end objective.

3. If the workers accept the evaluation but do not change as a result, you have not achieved the end objective.

TIP: How do you know if you will reach the end objective before you have wasted your time? A good place to start is by asking those affected: the workers. If they take negatively to your ideas, you might want to proceed cautiously.

EVERYBODY = NOBODY

A vision statement that applies to everybody, applies to nobody. This happens when you fail to define the vision.

1. The vision must be stated in precise terms and agreed upon by your team.

2. The vision must be desirable, and you must have some control over it. If you can't control it, your efforts will lack impact.

3. The vision must always be in view. Few people can find meaning in the journey alone without the promise or hope for something "better."

TIP: Update your team on its progress regularly. When evaluating how far you have come, avoid abstractions such as, "We are way ahead of where we were this time last month." Analyze your capacity for driving through and maintaining momentum for the long haul.

FACTS AND HYPOTHESES

The scientific method helps us establish a procedure for finding the facts about a particular issue.

1. A **fact** is a close agreement between competent observers of a series of observations of the same phenomenon.

2. A **hypothesis** is an educated guess; a reasonable explanation of an observation of experimental results that is not fully accepted as factual, but that can be used to guide us toward a fact.

3. The employee is probably the person with the greatest competence when it comes to determining whether or not he or she should embrace a particular procedure.

TIP: Before we can establish a new law in science, or a new policy (or fact) in the workplace, we must form a hypothesis. The problem is that we often tend to jump to conclusions based on the hypothesis without first doing sufficient experimentation. Although scientific principles are great teachers, when searching for the science (the discovery of evidence and relationships) all hypotheses (the predictions of the consequences) must be testable. In other words, for the predictions to be valid there must be a way of proving them wrong.

"The brightest flashes in the world of thought are incomplete until they have been proved to have their counterparts in the world of fact."

--John Tyndall (1820-1893 CE), British physicist

FEED THE TEAM FIRST

The team is built around the "I" concept. Identity, for example, involves more than wearing the uniform or mouthing a slogan. The "selfish" needs of the team must be satisfied before the needs of the customer can be satisfied.

1. When people want to work together, they will help each other and further contribute to the cohesiveness of the team.

2. Without team cohesiveness you don't have a team; each worker will be working alone. As a result customer service will suffer.

3. Feed the team first before feeding the customers to establish a sense of pride and ownership. The members of the team must feel their successes regularly and know that their opinions matter.

TIP: When selecting your team, select people who want to work with each other. Randomly grouping any number of people together does not make a team.

FEELING COOL

Feeling cool allows us to step a little outside of reality and live our dreams. But what is cool to me is not necessarily cool to you.

1. Go to the ski-hill, the beach, or the gym and observe how people dress and act. Some people feel cool dressing up, others feel cool dressing casual; some people like bright colors, others like earth tones, but we all want to feel cool.

2. If you could dress any way you wanted, what would you wear? If you could drive any car you wanted, what would you drive? Why?

3. When we feel cool, we are "in the zone," we are in tune with ourselves. When we are in tune with ourselves, we feel more natural; we are happier and prouder and perform better. We have an identity. We know who we are. This is the essence of teamwork.

TIP: How you perform has a lot to do with how you feel about yourself. Allow for some leeway in how you want your people to dress and act, in order that they may get in tune with themselves and feel cool.

FLAG TO DIE FOR

The American flag has 13 stripes and 50 stars. People *die* for the flag. Why?

1. People die for the flag because it symbolizes our identity; it's who we are. The stripes and stars have implications that extend far beyond the shape and colors of the flag.

2. A top-rated team is not a one-size-fits-all concept. This is the same idea that gives the Marines the right to call themselves "the few, the proud."

3. Pride comes from knowing that you are unique, stronger, and better than the competition. How you perform has a lot to do with your identity.

TIP: A flag, an emblem, a widget serve to unite a people. You raise the flag and pledge allegiance because you identify with it. Take a look at your company's widget. You have seen it a hundred times. If asked to describe it, and all you do is give the facts; its colors and shapes, you are missing the boat.

FOUR-LETTER WORDS

How many times have you heard, "Think positive and delete four-letter words, such as *can't* and *won't*"?

1. Getting hyped up only works for a short time. Real problems require real solutions.

2. To determine whether something is good or bad, we must relate it to what we wish to achieve. Four-letter words such as can't and won't do not automatically imply laziness, bad attitudes, or lack of confidence. Why should we all be extroverts? Perhaps silence is golden?

3. Do is not better than don't, can is not better than can't, proactive is not better than reactive, half-full is not better than half-empty, sunshine is not better than rain. If we desire to get rid of what's in the glass, we would much rather it be half-empty than half-full.

TIP: Support your ideas with concrete evidence and not abstract thought.

FREEING YOUR MIND OF CLUTTER

When you free your mind of clutter, you can ask the right questions that will guide you to the right answer. You can then speak the truth with conviction and inspire others to follow. But any search for truth requires skepticism.

1. Groupthink tends to occur within a group of people who are trying to reach a consensus without applying critical thought and analysis.

2. The dissenters, those who question your ideas, may be your most valuable employees because they counteract this groupthink mentality and help you achieve a more balanced perspective.

3. You can choose to grow your bad habits or your good habits for future generation leaders to study. Neither way necessarily requires more effort than the other, but it does require the wisdom to know the difference.

TIP: *The fact that your followers do not accept an atmosphere of strict obedience should be celebrated. If you can draw strength from their resourcefulness, you will welcome doubt without viewing it as an assault on your person. In fact, a healthy dose of talk and debate can have the effect of bringing down barriers, not raising them.*

GONE FISHIN'

Leadership follows the model for learning: rote, understanding, application, correlation.

1. **Rote.** You can repeat back information by memory without understanding or being able to apply the information properly.

2. **Understanding.** You can explain how and why, but cannot perform proficiently. Although proficiency in performance comes over a period of time and practice, proficient performance without understanding is mechanical and useless in a situation that requires you to adapt.

3. **Application.** You can use the skill and perform the tasks non-mechanically, and adapt by performing the tasks under less than predictable circumstances.

4. **Correlation.** You can see how the material *correlates* to other material you have not yet learned. You can use a skill intended for a specific task and apply it to another task without asking the help of others.

TIP: Application = Give a man a fish, and he will eat for a day. Correlation = Teach a man to fish, and he will eat for life. Go fishing every day.

HEARTS AND MINDS

Even though it is difficult to achieve your best by keeping things the same, you must consider how change affects others. Employees will more readily accept change if the idea originates with them and not with the supervisor or manager.

1. Successful leadership requires insight into human personality, which cannot be summarized in a simple saying posted on your office door.

2. Before implementing new ideas, you must first win the hearts and minds of your people.

3. No matter how great the idea is, unless others feel ownership they are not likely to support you. Just ask whose ideas you like the most: those that you come up with yourself or those that somebody else comes up with?

TIP: An honest evaluation a few weeks and again a few months after the change has been implemented will help guard against employee and customer dissatisfaction. If the change did not accomplish the desired results, fine-tune with employee input openly talked about and valued.

HISTORY LESSON

Throw a man in the river, and when his clothes have dried, he shall be the same as before.

1. History consists of a long row of less than pleasant events. Although we can always look back and say that a particular principle was sound or unsound, we cannot look forward with the same confidence.

2. When you have worked for a company for twenty years, you have no doubt been through the cycle of mistakes several times under different leadership—or even more frightening—under the *same* leadership.

3. We let passion rule over reason and frequently repeat mistakes that seem frighteningly similar to those made by generations of leaders long gone.

TIP: Look back over a period of a few years and try to find a pattern of leadership mistakes. If you fail to understand your mistakes, *as soon as your clothes have dried*, you shall be the same as before.

"No man ever steps in the same river twice, for it is not the same river and he is not the same man."

--Heraclitus (c. 535-475 BCE), ancient Greek philosopher

IF A TREE FALLS IN THE FOREST

Is sound objective or subjective? Or as the cliché goes: If a tree falls in the forest and nobody is there to hear it, will it make a sound? If you hold a briefing and nobody is there to hear you, does your speech have meaning?

1. The transmission of sound requires a medium, because if there is nothing to compress and expand there can be no sound.

2. The so-called grapevine is an example of how sound travels like a wave even to those who did not hear the original speaker.

3. The reflection of sound is called an **echo**. If the surfaces reflecting the sound are too reflective, however, the sound becomes garbled and you may not hear the sound as it was originally intended. This is what propagates the transmission of rumors.

TIP: If you have an audience, but they don't *want* to listen, they will hear only what they want to hear and not what is actually being said. Your job is not to make them listen, but to make them *want* to listen.

"I" IN TEAM

Although each part of a team has different qualities, the different parts can blend into a single unit. With this in mind, who stole "I" from team?

1. "There is no I in team," is one of the most overused and abused team sayings. No matter who you are or where you work, you will no doubt remember some sport coach, supervisor, or motivational speaker telling you just this. No doubt will you remember somebody's calendar posted on somebody's office wall displaying this particular slogan.

2. Why should we care about no "I" in team if we don't also have some way of associating ourselves with the deeper meaning of teamwork? The saying is in principle as meaningful (or meaningless) as describing the American flag as thirteen stripes for the original states and fifty stars for the current states. Who cares about the stars and the stripes, if we don't also have some way of associating ourselves with the meaning of our flag?

3. The team does not work for the customer. Each team member works for the other members on the team. The reason why is because it is the team and not the customer who gives the members their identity.

4. Just as molecules vary in strength and contain a combination of properties, a functional team must be varied and strong and contain a combination of qualities including those that are complex and those that are simple.

TIP: Good customer service is a byproduct of a well-run team. If you want good customer service you must first fix the team.

INTELLECTUAL GROWTH

The ability to properly discern relationships is often the result of an enormous amount of knowledge.

1. Intellectual growth comes from the encouragement of open-minded debate, not from the memorization of and ability to restate principles.

2. A system that is so rigid that it makes no allowances for human emotions tends to make leadership principles meaningless.

3. When you refrain from shielding yourself from those opposing your ideas and instead strive to understand them in the proper context, you will set yourself up for intellectual growth.

TIP: Study leadership with a critical eye. It is almost impossible to rate efficiency based on physical characteristics and educational background of an employee. You must also study human emotions.

IN THE EYE OF THE BEHOLDER

Whether a change is good or bad is often in the eye of the beholder.

1. People are individuals and, although the employees who work under you may be a team, it is their individualism that gives the team its strength.

2. Adopting a positive attitude is a superficial and overly simplistic solution to dealing with change. Real problems, such as the loss of one's job and livelihood, require real solutions and not just a "good attitude."

3. Believing that you can teach people to like change, or stop "hemming and hawing" and "just move with the cheese," suggests either careless or arrogant thinking.

TIP: Employees are more willing to change when they recognize that there is an advantage to changing. Before asking for change, the intelligent and critical leader makes an absolutely honest assessment of his or her true reason for desiring change, and questions if the change will truly bring improvement.

IN THE FISHBOWL

When dealing with people, sometimes common sense trumps scientific evidence.

1. When human emotions are involved, all logic is not true and all truth is not logic.

2. How the employees feel about the leader and a particular issue often determines whether or not they will cooperate and follow.

3. Passion often overrules logic and scientific evidence, and action must be guided by appropriate recognition of feelings.

TIP: *Before you can repair a problem you must repair the damaged emotions of the employees. Remember that you are in the fishbowl; you are on stage for those you lead.*

IN THE TRENCHES

It has been said that leadership mistakes made in the planning are the most difficult to forgive, because it often means that those affected are doomed before they even start. But since leadership theoreticians don't deal with the complex problems of life in the trenches, how do you guard against stumbling into the wrong trench?

1. Start by going a step beyond the obvious and taking possession of what you hear and see.

2. Comment and question and speak of what you know from experience and gut feeling.

3. Seek support from a team that is extraordinarily able and committed.

4. Dissect the meaning of every problem and ask as many questions pertaining to the scenario as possible.

5. Acknowledge the fact that being politically correct often blurs one's vision.

6. Challenge yourself to see things as they are, not as you wish them to be, and do what is right.

TIP: Practicing leadership means that you must actively seek out opportunities that help you improve your leadership skills.

I OWN, YOU OWN

If the team lacks the physical resources or carries a load of mental baggage, you must choose a better time for presenting a motivating principle.

1. Motivation needs reinforcement. To build natural enthusiasm, the team must be reminded of the motivating factor.

2. Motivation needs approval. A skillful leader can build enthusiasm by helping the individual perform successfully in front of his or her peers.

3. Motivation needs a goal. "Every day is a great day," or, "Be happy that you're alive," or, "Do something today that makes a customer smile," are weak motivators. Tangible goals heighten awareness and curiosity.

TIP: Goals should be neither too lofty, nor too simple. Remind your team of the rewards. Motivation needs ownership. This is why it matters who gets the credit.

ISSUES OF PASSION

With few exceptions most conflicts are issues of passion. Even wars and world events are often issues of passion and not necessity.

1. A team leader can be passionate about an issue, but the employees can be equally passionate about the reciprocal.

2. Issues of passion can easily become a matter of who is right rather than what is right.

3. People have emotions and when their emotions are upset they are not likely to respond to anything the leader says.

TIP: Understanding the emotional part of human nature, no matter how illogical, may be the most important part related to success in leadership. People excel when they have a passion for the job.

IT'S RAINING

A character trait is seldom good or bad by itself; it depends on how the person uses it.

1. Teaching physical skills is easier than teaching mental, social, or leadership skills such as self-control, communication, and patience.

2. It's not your personality traits that determine your leaderships skills, but what you *do* with these personality traits. Being patient or impatient, outspoken or quiet, opinionated or flexible, energetic or laid back can be either good or bad.

3. It's raining! Good or bad, positive or negative? If you are having a picnic for your daughter's tenth birthday and it's raining, then somebody literally "rained on your parade." But if you are a farmer battling months of draught, you will be delighted at the rainfall.

TIP: Evaluate how the team impacts your day-to-day activities. When you get the urge to slap a "bad" label on something that somebody says or does, take the time to examine why.

JUST A NUMBER

Efficient teamwork is about developing the qualities you find in each team member, and not trying to make each member what he or she is not.

1. The reason why a large team has a greater potential to be a motivation killer than a small team, is because each member on a large team tends to become only a number. In other words, individual identity is lost.

2. In a large team each member will be shielded from pain and the effects of wrongdoing, and can therefore not feel a great sense of ownership.

3. Specific responsibilities cannot be delegated in a team that is too large, because we assume that "it is everybody's responsibility," and everybody's responsibility becomes nobody's responsibility.

TIP: A good guideline when contemplating team size is to start by defining the tasks the team needs to accomplish and the number of members needed for each task.

KNOW WHERE YOU ARE GOING

The leader takes the team to the finish line—safely. He is respected for his courage and honesty, even when he is the carrier of bad news.

1. The leader's role might be the most important in any business, team, or group, because the leader takes an interest in the mission, the objective, *and* the team.

2. A good leader ensures that the future is not a guess game. Uncertainty brings more stress than bad news, not only when one's livelihood or safety is at stake but also with respect to trivial everyday issues.

3. Moving forward without a leader is like writing a book by copying the words of others, or like going to school without a teacher. Somebody must tell us how far we have come. The best leader can take the team beyond his or her own limitations.

TIP: What's in a word? Are you a mentor, a supervisor, a facilitator, a mediator, or a leader? Each word has certain connotations. Explain how you want to be perceived by your team and management, and why?

LESSON IN LOGIC AND TRUTH

When you know the truth and see the evidence, you have no problem foregoing debate and accepting the conclusion. This is the essence of logic argumentation.

1. If A=B and B=C, then A=C. The fundamental principle of logic states: "If the premises (the examples that set it up) are true, the conclusion will automatically follow."

2. The same does not apply to human emotions: If **A**dam loves **B**ridgette and **B**ridgette loves **C**hristopher, then **A**dam loves **C**hristopher. Although this could be true, it is most likely false. When human emotions are involved, all logic is not true, and all truth is not logic.

3. Before you do the calculations, step back and ask, "What would make sense?" After you have done the calculations, step back and ask, "Does it make sense?"

TIP: Set up a relationship that automatically leads to the truth. Define and agree on the premises with your team. Ask, "Does it make sense?"

LIKING THINGS THE WAY THEY ARE

A common reason for negative reactions toward change is that people feel secure in their present positions and like things "the way they are." Another reason is lack of information about the change. Nobody likes coming to work only to discover that their "map" no longer matches their surroundings.

1. Having the opportunity to do the things they are good at and enjoy will make each team member more likely to come to work with a good attitude, excel, be productive, look for solutions to problems, and less likely to take excessive sick days.

2. Barriers are not necessarily broken by cross-utilizing employees and forcing them to work in areas where they do not want to work. This sort of behavior is more likely to cause discontent, lack of productivity, and more sick days.

3. How big a part your employees can play in problem solving and how secure they feel at work is directly related to how much information they receive.

TIP: Before implementing change, consider it in view of the ideas that emerged during discussion and brainstorming sessions with your employees. During the implementation stage of the change, those affected must get the full support of management, and management must be open to further suggestions for fine-tuning the change.

LIMITED SCOPE OF THE MIND

A principle may be a starting point as long as it is open to critique. When employees are allowed to critique widely, we eliminate much subjectivity and decrease the risk that we might use the limited scope of a single leader's mind as a standard.

1. A problem with many leadership slogans is that they tell us what the goal is without giving specific examples of what needs to be done.

2. If you fail to define, you will also fail to communicate clearly. When you fail to communicate, it will be difficult to get others to agree. And when you cannot reach agreement, your mission will likely fail.

3. You do not have to do everything that your team is asking of you, but you do have to understand it.

TIP: You cannot be all to everybody. In other words, don't be a cosmic clause. It is better to stand for one thing than to stand for everything.

MADE OR BORN?

Good leaders are made, not born . . . or is it the other way around?

1. The leader gains the support of the members of his or her team by knowing what makes them tick.

2. The leader who understands others modifies his or her leadership skills to accommodate the individuals that make up the team.

3. A good leader practices leadership consistently and with intent, performs realistic self-evaluations, and consciously tries to adopt the characteristics of a good leader.

TIP: Present the belief that the goals are achievable, but don't be gung-ho. Most people are not interested in changing who they are or wandering too far from their comfort zone.

MATTER OF TIMING

When a team performs without the leader's verbal guidance, it is in tune with the leader and the goal. The leader has then fulfilled the communication requirement without the need to be excessively verbal.

1. People have emotions, and when they are upset, they are not likely to respond to what you have to say.

2. People don't listen or change when they are threatened or forced to do so. You must invite them in and meet them halfway.

3. The transmitter must be ready, willing, and able to communicate the message. The receiver must be ready, willing, and able to receive the message.

4. If we are concerned only with ourselves, we will say only what we want to say and hear only what we want to hear.

TIP: Time a message right by understanding that people are people first, before they are agents, workers, or employees.

MORAL COURAGE

Just as physical courage may be the first characteristic of good generalship on the battlefield, moral courage is the first characteristic of good leadership in the civilian world.

1. Reality in leadership is often what your gut tells you and not what you wish for, nor what some mathematical equation or scientific principle suggests.

2. The logic of leadership is grounded in empirical evidence of right or wrong behavior, and, yes, the leader must face a level of personal risk.

3. A good leader is the assistant to the team and is simultaneously at the mercy of the team. He gives the team the benefit of the doubt while risking the mistakes and blunders.

TIP: Take full responsibility for your actions and for the actions of your team.

MUTUAL EXCLUSIVITY

Although complex makes strong, in science some of the simplest molecules like water and oxygen are also the most life sustaining. How is it in leadership? Just how complex should your team be?

1. A team can be viewed as a complex organism whose total strength rests in the differences and not in the similarities between individuals.

2. When the bonds between individuals break due to too much "steam," the team will become unstable and unable to function as a unit.

3. If too little heat is applied, all energy is withdrawn and the team will lose motivation and become lethargic.

TIP: A fully functioning team must have members with complementary qualities. **Complementary** means "mutually exclusive." This concept can be likened to how one part, branch, or department of a company cannot function without another.

NOTHING TO COMPLAIN ABOUT

There is a difference between being "bossy" and being a leader. The leader must be there for his or her team when they need him no matter what the situation.

1. If you delegate responsibility for a task that was previously yours, such as scheduling (even if the employees ask for it), it does not give you authority to hold out your hands and say, "Hey, you got what you wanted," when they complain.

2. Passing the buck does not relieve you of responsibility. Passing the buck is like running over a bicyclist with your car and saying that it was not your fault that he died because he was not wearing a helmet!

3. Defining the steps along the way is important because definitions provide expectations of what the team will accomplish and open the door for questions and debate, which further aid the leader in fine-tuning the journey and help him avoid as many obstacles as possible.

TIP: The value of an idea lies in the substance and not in the words. Be specific and not general in your definition if you want your ideas to have meaning. To take ownership of an idea, you must carry a thought to conclusion.

NUMBER 10 AND WHY SIZE MATTERS

If the team needs 9 members to function and you are number 10, you are the one they don't need. If the team needs 10 members to function and you are number 10, you are the piece that makes the puzzle whole.

1. A properly functioning team helps us find our strengths, eradicate our fears, and beat the odds at a rate that is greater than proportional to the size of the team.

2. The smaller the team, the more maneuverable and flexible it is. Trying to make a large team conform to a single set of standards takes time and effort and reduces efficiency. Bigger is not necessarily better, and over-staffing may be worse than under-staffing. Size is a fine line to walk.

3. A team is not any group of people. Team and company are not synonymous. Your company can comprise several teams.

TIP: Make the team small enough that no member is expendable, and specific enough to bring about feelings of pride and ownership.

OH, DID I TELL YOU I TOOK SECOND PLACE?

Taking second place is meaningless, unless you know how many people are in the race. When we lack tangible evidence to measure ourselves against, we also lack knowledge of where to place our next step.

1. If two people are in the race, taking second place is not particularly admirable. If a thousand people are in the race, taking second place is pretty darn good.

2. Meaningless: "All positions reviewed receive competitive pay and benefits in comparison to their peer groups in the rest of the industry." Define *competitive* in concrete terms.

3. Meaningless: "Each workgroup reviewed ranks near the top of the industry, and is projected to rank number 2 or 3 by the end of the year." Is number 2 or 3 good or bad? How many workgroups are in the race?

TIP: State in writing what you have done today, this week, or this month that placed you a step closer to achieving your vision. A word of caution: Stating what you have done this week is useless, unless you also show how it helps bring you closer to achieving the vision. Think the thought to conclusion.

OPEN VERSUS CLOSED DOORS

When you know how to ask and answer questions, can you hear the talk? Conflicts are not necessarily bad but become so when you fail to understand the essential issue.

1. When a conflict is handled properly, it will increase your confidence and deepen your thinking. Most managers say they have an "open door policy," yet many employees do not feel they can take advantage of it, because whenever they come with an issue to discuss, it is immediately shot down.

2. Having an open door policy does not automatically make the manager more "approachable" even if he is "available." If people are uncomfortable talking with you, it will not matter how "open" your door is, they will stop coming to you with suggestions or ideas.

3. Do not accept a challenge to prove a point. Keep sensitive issues behind closed doors and remember that people are people first before they are agents, workers, or employees.

TIP: When times are bad, it is fruitless to remind your team that they should be happy they have a job at all. People have emotions, and when they are upset they are not likely to respond to what you have to say.

OPTIMIZED TEAM

Cross-utilization does not produce an optimized team. A team that is supposedly optimized through cross-utilization will likely be no team at all.

1. When cross-utilizing the workforce, what is supposed to bring the employees together will instead have the opposite effect of sabotaging the team concept. Many employees will no longer know exactly what is expected of them. Many will no longer feel competent, and with the focus on (team) optimization rather than individual excellence, many employees will no longer feel validated or important.

2. People excel when they have the opportunity to fine-tune and perfect their skills in one specific area. When selecting your team, look for varied abilities between individuals, rather than for varied abilities within a person.

3. One of the core concepts of a cohesive team is this: The team members must WANT to form a team; a team is not just ANY group of people. People who like each other and want to work together should therefore be placed together.

TIP: When you have hired people to perform a specific job and suddenly ask them to do another job or take on additional duties not in their job description, the reason why you run into difficulties may be because the people you hired are specialists in their specific areas, and asking them to do other types of jobs means that you are capitalizing on their weaknesses and not on their strengths.

ORGANIZING YOUR THOUGHTS

Science is about discovering evidence and relationships for observable phenomena, and establishing theories that organize and make sense of those phenomena. **Technology** is about the tools, techniques, and procedures we use for implementing the scientific findings.

1. If we know the principles but do not have the capacity to utilize them, we are not very successful as leaders.

2. The opposite is also true. If we apply the technology, the methods and techniques, but do not understand the underlying principles, we may end up using the wrong tools and be unable to perform the job satisfactorily.

3. There are a number of steps that must be followed: Recognize that there is a problem, make an educated guess and predict the consequences (form a hypothesis), perform experiments to test the predictions, and formulate the simplest general rule that organizes the hypothesis and experimental outcome into a theory.

TIP: Use the principles of science and the tools of technology to organize your thoughts in the proper sequence and decrease the risk of making mistakes.

"Skill already developed may be refined by the study of past examples, but skill is only acquired in actually dealing with present examples."

--Carl von Clausewitz (1780-1831 CE), Prussian military theorist

PAYOFF

How do you move people to action?

1. Popular passion is necessary, of course, particularly when personal sacrifice is needed. Ideals must pay off on personal terms.

2. If there is no payoff, the leader is merely engaging in self-serving interests and cannot expect the team to follow willingly.

3. Sometimes the leader's job is to create popular passion and motivate the team to accept a change that in the leader's mind will lead to greater results; or as is so often stated, to work smarter but not harder. But why should the team want to work smarter? What is the payoff?

TIP: If you reward the team for working smarter with longer breaks, or perhaps even allow them to go home early with full pay, they will inevitably find a way to work smarter.

PRESERVING THE HUNGER

People are not inherently lazy. Most of us want to work and enjoy contributing with our ideas for the purpose of increasing the efficiency of our organization.

1. Whether or not games and friendly competition are good motivators is an individual issue. What motivates you may be a turnoff to me, and vice versa. Our ideas of "fun" differ.

2. The people you lead are motivated to succeed through the power of your motivation. If your motivation stems from personal success that does not include the team, then why should they follow if they can't share in the rewards?

3. Motivation may be our strongest driving force. To remain hungry and receptive to motivation, the team must realize the value of the task it is attempting to accomplish.

TIP: Respect that people are different. Identify what motivates the members on your team by asking them individually. Preserve the hunger by relating the value of the task to the individual wishes and desires.

PROPER THINKING

All sources of information are valuable to the leader, but few are as valuable as those that help you use your knowledge to guide others.

1. Although specific techniques for performing a task can be taught, concepts are more difficult to teach.

2. Intelligence is demonstrated through an understanding of the concepts and not through repetition of techniques, nor through the mindless repetition of popular slogans.

3. Part of leadership encompasses mechanics of technique; the other part encompasses proper thinking.

TIP: *Next time you observe a member of your team using a different technique than the one called for when accomplishing a specific task, rather than correcting him or her, ask why.*

PROVERBIAL SHIT

Heat (like the proverbial shit) flows only one way: downhill from hot to cold. This is why, when the supervisor takes "heat" from his superiors, the employees will surely take heat from the supervisor in the near future.

1. If not managed, organized systems will eventually decay and descend into chaos; that is unless the system is open and allows for proper transfer of energy.

2. Every change you implement that is perceived by the team in negative terms will create a slight loss from the "original."

3. When a team is allowed to break apart, it takes more energy to restore its original shape than the amount of energy that was lost through entropy. This is why first impressions are important and why it is difficult to remedy a leadership faux pas.

TIP: If many years pass where there is no inflow of energy, or no motivation, the workforce will become lethargic. By contrast, when you add energy to a system such as a team, it can convert that energy to a different form and produce work that helps the company achieve the desired goals. The trick is to add the right kind and the right amount of energy.

READY TO PEAK

The main obstacle to motivation is lack of desire. Others include:

1. Unfair treatment or critique. Fairness does not necessarily mean that everybody is treated exactly the same, and critique is not in itself an obstacle to motivation. In fact, it could be a catalyst, but the person critiqued must understand and agree with the critique.

2. Leader lack of interest, or appearing uninterested even if you are interested. If you have other things on your mind, you must still appear interested in front of your team or explain the reasons for your apparent lack of interest.

3. Physical discomfort or illness. A person who is sick or carries mental baggage must satisfy his or her personal needs first. As someone once said, "If it ain't right at home, it ain't right at work, either."

4. Apathy caused by inadequate preparation or inability to organize. Leader inability to take the efforts of the team seriously is a contributor to apathy.

5. Change. When change occurs, more than one person is affected. All those affected by the change must therefore know that their feelings are respected. Including your team in discussions for change can help alleviate this obstacle.

TIP: *The team must be ready to peak in order to peak. If the team lacks the necessary physical resources or carries significant mental baggage, choose a better time for presenting the motivating factor.*

REALITY VERSUS PASSION

A leader who is so passionate about an idea that it brings him to tears may momentarily touch some hearts, but he will rarely win the minds of his team without demonstrating the will to inconvenience himself for his cause.

1. The leader's first responsibility when attempting to express a vision, solve a problem, reach a consensus, and lead the team toward the goal is to define reality.

2. The leader's gut feeling must be balanced by logic and intellect, curiosity and maturity, open-mindedness and self-reflection.

3. The leader must think critically, encourage response, and avoid getting trapped in meaningless sayings.

TIP: Although leadership books and popular slogans such as, "Today is the first day of the rest of your life," or, "Half-full is better than half-empty," can aid thinking, when reality contradicts theory, you should go with reality.

RESISTANCE TO CHANGE

When you try to implement change, there *will* be inertia.

1. Implementing change in the workplace is difficult when you need to convince a large group of people of your views, particularly if these people are already opposed to your views. You must not only stop their current motion which is directing them away from your views, you must also start motion in a new direction.

2. Change in direction means a change in momentum because a component part of the momentum equation is **velocity**, or speed and direction.

3. An alternative to stopping the motion or slowing it down when desiring to change the momentum is to change the direction through the application of an outside force.

TIP: When you exert a force in the workplace, you create an *interaction* between yourself and the person against whom you exert the force. It is unreasonable to think that you can exert a force against a person without also expecting to feel the effects of that force.

"We would rather be ruined than changed; we would rather die in our dread, than climb the cross of the moment and let our illusions die."

--Wystan Hugh Auden (1907-1973 CE), British-born American poet

REWARD AND PUNISHMENT

Rewarding good behavior is honorable. But doing nothing when punishment is called for is as bad as being too harsh.

1. By doing nothing, you are in effect failing to reinforce good behavior while giving quiet approval of bad behavior.

2. By failing to punish bad behavior, you are in effect punishing the good workers for their good behavior. Then why would any worker want to work smarter?

3. Build on people's strengths and not on their weaknesses. Reward not only good behavior but good outcomes.

TIP: Avoid punishing good behavior by rewarding bad. You will not make a right-handed person more efficient at writing by forcing him or her to use the left hand.

RIGHT FROM THE BEGINNING

Science is fascinating not because of the discoveries but because of the predictability; finding that the truth is in fact logic and steadfast, and that the concepts that were true a thousand years ago are still true today and most likely will be true tomorrow.

1. The leader who knows the truth and sees the evidence will have no problem foregoing debate and accepting the conclusion. He or she can enjoy the benefit of doing things right from the beginning.

2. Science involves the discovery of evidence and relationships; it demonstrates why things work the way they do.

3. Technology gives us the tools and procedures. Science gives us a clear field of vision. Technology allows us to pursue our goals without second-guessing the outcome of our actions.

TIP: The careful observer, whether supervisor or employee, will do himself and the team a service by carefully analyzing how he applies scientific analogies to team leadership.

ROOM FOR IMPROVEMENT?

The idea that we can motivate people through euphemisms, or simply by assigning a positive meaning to a word, such as "there is always room for improvement," is disingenuous.

1. Unless we have analyzed and measured in some tangible way exactly what needs to be done and how it will improve the current situation, saying that there is always room for improvement becomes rather meaningless.

2. Change does not automatically bring improvement and doing more (or doing something) is not necessarily a measure of success.

3. Real problems require real solutions, and whether the glass is half-full or half-empty is a matter of which direction the contents are flowing. If it is being filled, it is half-full; if it is being emptied, it is half-empty. If we don't know whether it is being filled or emptied, we don't have enough information to answer the question of whether it is half-full or half-empty.

TIP: Motivation comes through a desire to achieve something that has real value, and not through positive or negative commands.

"Every great scientific truth goes through three stages. First, people say it conflicts with the Bible; next, they say it has been discovered before; lastly, they say they always believed it."

--Louis Agassiz (1807-1873 CE), Swiss-born American naturalist

SCIENTIFIC METHOD

If you don't see what others see, you may make false assumptions. The *scientific method* is a good place to start, because it sort of covers your bases. How does it work?

1. Recognize that there is a problem. If you don't know that you have a problem, it will be difficult to resolve it. Then make an educated guess. The guess must be reasonably related to the problem.

2. Predict the consequences. This is called forming a *hypothesis.* When you have made an educated guess, forming the hypothesis is easier. Then test the hypothesis to determine if your educated guess has merit and your prediction is valid.

3. Formulate a rule as simple and straight forward as possible, intended to correct the problem.

TIP: It is easy to fall prey to our own capacity to fool ourselves. When analyzing problems, learn to distinguish between what you see and what you wish to see. Be ready to accept your findings, even if they are not what you wish them to be.

SITTING ON TWO CHAIRS

It has been said that if you try to sit on two chairs at the same time, you will most likely fall in-between.

1. Know on which chair you sit and face the truth with courage and honor.

2. When you share information or discuss new policies with your people, state the truth—all of it. If you withhold certain facts, you will be perceived as unreliable and dishonest.

3. Bring information into the open, even when you are the carrier of bad news. Secrecy invites speculation and the flow of rumors. Bad news, when told with sincerity and clear-sightedness, will be taken in stride by the workers.

TIP: It is better with an honest foe than an inconsistent friend; at least you know what you've got.

SITUATIONAL AWARENESS

To end up where you want to go, you must first know where you are; you must have "situational awareness."

1. Not liking what you have, but not knowing what you want makes navigation difficult. Place two Xs on the map: Where are you? Where are you going? How do you get there?

2. Everybody on the team must have the same vision. Pursuing the vision alone is meaningless. Lack of clear communication = alone.

3. When considering the objective, also consider the means of travel: your team. How will the journey affect your team, your company, the customer, and the competition? How will it affect your relationship to your superiors and subordinates?

TIP: Defining the vision makes it less intimidating and allows you to view it with a clear eye. Take the first step, but also think about what might be the last.

SIZE VERSUS STRENGTH

A balance must be struck between the small and big team.

1. It is not only important how big something is, but also in what direction it is moving. As the size of an object increases, the object grows heavier much faster than it grows stronger.

2. Bigger does not necessarily translate into stronger. A team has an optimum size that allows it to function as a unit where members can bond properly and avoid wasting energy.

3. A team with too many similar qualities between its members will be less strong, than a team with unlike but complementary qualities.

TIP: Each group must complement the others to form a whole, or what we call a workable and efficient team.

SMARTER, NOT HARDER

There is a difference between working hard and being productive. Good leaders avoid wasting time. But how do you know that "smarter" is better than "harder?"

1. Good leaders question, experiment, and research; good leaders are farsighted and balanced and look beyond the moment.

2. Good leaders have a solid understanding of the forces that confront them—the forces inherent in their team and the forces of the competition.

3. Good leaders are imaginative and creative in their thinking; they pave the way through definite steps that the team can clearly see.

TIP: Good leaders are interested in furthering their education and growing the strength of the team. But what is your team interested in? What are the risks associated with being too creative?

SPOTTING A LEADER

A leader has command presence. You know when a leader walks into the room, because he fills the space and you can feel it.

1. Spotting a leader by his or her looks is difficult. Spotting a leader by his or her demeanor is easy.

2. Character and strength may be the most important leadership qualities. The leader needs character in order to gain the support of his team; he needs strength in order to carry the mission to completion.

3. Although leaders should be compensated for their efforts, the best leaders are in it for the journey and not for a hidden agenda or material payoff.

TIP: Why does a writer write? Because he has something to say. Why does a bird sing? Because it has a song. Why does a leader lead?

STEPPINGSTONES

Remember that you *must* win. Being the best that you can be is meaningless if the competition is better.

1. Simply hanging inspirational posters on the wall, and including a line or two in your vision statement about integrity and dazzling customer service does not make it so.

2. A problem with many motivational sayings is that nobody explains how to use them.

3. To prove meaningful, the vision must be agreed upon and achievable within a reasonable time.

TIP: Present two or three definite steps rather than a list of twenty concepts. Rather than striving to become the greatest, you might want to state a slightly less valuable, yet more precise and achievable goal, knowing that it is a steppingstone toward the loftier vision.

"Climb if you will, but remember that courage and strength are naught without prudence, and a momentary negligence may destroy the happiness of a lifetime."

-- Edward Whymper (1840-1911 CE), British climber and explorer

STRATEGY AND TACTICS

Few people will find meaning in the journey alone, with no promise or hope of a reward at the end of the tunnel. The same goes for your vision. If you cannot list the steps required to get there (wherever "there" is), the vision will have little value.

1. Strategy is your plan and tactics are the particular steps you take, or the means you use to realize your strategy.

2. If you have a strategy but no tactics, your vision will remain on the drawing table; it will never be realized.

3. If you have tactics but no strategy, your vision will become a trial and error type endeavor.

TIP: When evaluating how far you have come, be precise and avoid abstract words such as "we can" or "we know." Do not say, "We are way ahead of where we were this time last month." Give the team concrete evidence instead.

TANGIBLE RETURNS

Motivation needs a concrete goal. Saying that "every day is a great day," or that you should "do something today that makes a customer smile," are weak motivators.

1. Tangible goals heighten awareness and curiosity. Your team must also want to win. This may seem obvious, but if the team members cannot care less whether they win or lose, not much will get done.

2. Rather than assuming that we all want to win, the question you should ask is this: What motivates the team to want to win? If winning does not come with a reward of some sort, if it carries no greater weight than losing, then why should the employees put forth the extra effort it takes to win?

3. How do you define winning? Does everybody on the team agree with the definition?

TIP: Tangible returns that are meaningful, such as a bonus or an extra day off with pay, carry greater weight than intangible returns such as a "thank you"; although, a "thank you" is nice, too, and is part of common courtesy.

TEAM DISCRIMINATION

The team must discriminate by including individuals who contribute to the strength of the team while excluding freeloaders.

1. A successful team contains **identity**, or the unique need of the individual to be part of the team. Identity is established through team colors, songs, uniforms, slogans, and widgets.

2. **Individualism** is the ability of each member to experience the value he or she brings to the team. Although individualism should be encouraged rather than dampened, it must still be managed.

3. **Size** is directly related to how well the team can function as a unit. A team that is too large will prevent the members from feeling ownership, and a team that is too small will prevent the members from functioning efficiently.

TIP: If the relationship between the different parts is not honed the unit will fail. If the unit fails, each individual part (team member) will also fail.

THEREFORE I AM

The leader cannot exist without the followers. The opposite is not necessarily true. The followers can benefit from a leader's direction and wisdom, but they do not need him or her to exist.

1. The leader's job is to figure out what makes the team tick. Goals, therefore, cannot solely be the company's goals or the manager's goals; they must be the team's goals and as such the goals of each individual member of the team.

2. The leader's repute is not determined solely by the job he performs or by the company for which he works. You can be a supervisor, a boss, or a dictator; you can inspire fear, threaten, coerce, and blackmail; you can sweet talk and bribe; but you can lead only if you have a following.

3. The ability to know how to think rather than what to think may be the leader's greatest asset. Learning how to think involves a conscious element of skepticism. It requires awareness of biases related to previous experiences, strong personal views, or current ambitions.

TIP: Understanding the relationship between leader and follower places the role of the leader in the proper perspective. You exist because of the team; not the other way around.

THINKING THE THOUGHT TO CONCLUSION

It is easier to be a yeah-sayer than to think the thought to conclusion.

1. **Intelligence** prevents the leader from misjudging situations that place the team in danger or ridicule. And **integrity** contributes to the cohesiveness of the team.

2. The leader does not own the team physically, mentally, or emotionally. Once everybody understands this, the leader can with good conscience lead the team toward the goal.

3. Although the ideal is something to live, fight, and sometimes even die for, our pride needs constant reinforcement to remain a motivating force.

TIP: How do you create a winning team? Use intelligence and common sense. Establish yourself as credible through integrity, or truthfulness and honesty.

TO HELL AND BACK

It's not the job that motivates the members of the team, but how they *feel* about the job. A good leader can motivate his or her team to follow him to hell and back. Motivational factors must:

1. Be challenging. Your team should feel a sense of accomplishment and pride. But goals must also be achievable.

2. Be desirable. Your team should feel the value of the achievement. The achievement must be meaningful. How do you know that it has meaning to the members of your team? You ask them.

3. Preserve the hunger. Your team will perform best when it is ready and eager to perform. Think timing.

4. Have duration. *"For one swallow does not make a summer . . ."*

TIP: Getting the team ready is your job. Identify the resources your team needs, and pay attention to how your team responds.

TOP OF THE MOUNTAIN

Not all paths lead to the top of the mountain but, most certainly, more than one path does.

1. The best way is often the way that suits the person who does the job. Everybody can do some things better than everybody else. A person who has a special skill and gets to use it will feel special and motivated. Growth and the elimination of weaknesses are not synonymous.

2. Telling somebody what to do is easy; telling them how to do it is difficult. Stating the facts is easy; bringing insight into the facts is difficult. Pointing out what is wrong is easy; knowing how to fix it is difficult.

3. Beyond defining the steps, good leadership requires the ability to "read between the lines," to see what is *not* there. Leadership is more about *how* to travel the road than which road to take.

TIP: Understanding the subtleties of individuals can help you place a person in a position where he or she will perform the strongest. Look for ways to capitalize on the strengths and passions of each member of your team, instead of eliminating their weaknesses.

TRANSMITTING THE MESSAGE

When you convey a new idea to your team, their attitudes may indicate resistance, passivity, or an unwillingness to comply. Barriers to communication include:

1. Lack of common experience. Understanding the team's background helps you determine the approach to take when communicating.

2. Lack of commitment or lack of trust. How the transmitter of the message and the receiver feel during the exchange has an impact on how the message is perceived.

3. Physical and mental discomfort. When either the transmitter or the receiver is grouchy, ill, or uncomfortable, the message may not be transmitted or received as intended, or may not be received at all.

4. Argumentation. Recognize an invitation to argue and avoid it. Consider how your team will view you if you accept an argument openly. Note that argumentation is not synonymous with debate or discussion.

TIP: Leadership = communication.

TRUTH VERSUS RUMOR

When you know something about communication, the final test is your ability to communicate the whole truth.

1. If an employee asks about his future with the company and you give him a vague answer like, "There are opportunities for growth and development," what has he learned? Absolutely nothing!

2. When the truth is spoken, it challenges people to get involved and creates commitment and team spirit. Withholding the truth creates insecurity.

3. Lack of truthful communication challenges the workers to find the information through their own reasoning—through rumors.

TIP: Rumors, faulty information, and worry steal energy from the workforce. Thus when you share information or discuss new policies with your people, state the truth, all of it. If you withhold certain facts, you will be perceived as unreliable and dishonest.

VERY DOES NOT MAKE IT MORE SO

Failing to define the vision and the steps is as uninspiring as saying that you are headed toward the goal. *What* goal? Each step is a prerequisite for the next, and not an entity in itself.

1. Very does not make it more so. How good do we want to be? We want to be *very* good. Upon reaching the vision, we want our customers to be *very* happy. We also want our employees to be *very* happy. Very has a different meaning to different people. How rich do you want to be? I want to be *very* rich. What does *very* mean?

2. If your vision is to "nurture and encourage the (your company's name) culture," or to "find creative, new, and efficient ways of doing business," explain what the culture is and how to be creative.

3. If your vision is to "be the biggest in the industry," or to "be the customer's number one choice," explain what the customer wants, and how you know this is what they want.

TIP: Meaningless or hard to define sayings add confusion between the leader and the team. When you have stated what should be done, state how you arrived at the conclusion. Then state how it should be done.

WHAT *CAN YOU DO?*

To determine whether something is good or bad, we must relate it to what we wish to achieve.

1. Your people could do a better job, *if* they wanted to. Your duty is not to make them do a better job, but to make them *want* to do a better job.

2. Although a job that presents opportunities for initiative and growth can enrich your life, an individual who is not motivated by competition, or personal praise, or teamwork, or free tickets to a football game, will not respond to such grand plans.

3. Everybody does not respond to the same type of motivation. If you want to use motivation to catapult your employees upward, you must also understand their passions, loves, goals, and desires.

TIP: When somebody says, "I can't do that," instead of saying, "Sure you can," or, "You are so negative," ask, "What *can* you do?"

WHAT IS, WHAT COULD HAVE BEEN

An evaluation must be objective. What is objective? It should not be based on personal opinion of performance. In other words, if somebody else had made the same observations of a particular employee's performance, he should have given a similar critique.

1. An evaluation or critique should not be based on whether or not you, the person administering the critique, like the person you are critiquing. Your mood on the particular day should not interfere. If you give the critique tomorrow, it should be the same as if you give it today. You must also base the critique on the actual performance that took place and not on what could have been.

2. The critique must be flexible to the degree that it fits the particular person, times, and circumstances that you are critiquing. It should not be taken out of context.

3. If the individual receiving the critique does not agree, or at least accept it, it is worthless. A critique should not be an opportunity to voice your dissatisfaction with the individual you are critiquing.

TIP: For the employee to accept the critique, it is essential that the person administering the critique is an authority on the subject. The fact that you are wearing a team leader patch does not alone qualify you to give an effective and acceptable critique.

WHAT, WHERE, HOW, AND WHY

Communication is an active process that requires participation. Communication involves listening and understanding the other person's perceptions, which requires interaction between the speaker and the listener.

1. Active listeners ask questions rather than finding something to argue about; they paraphrase the information to increase their understanding of what is being said.

2. Passive listeners have already decided beforehand what they want to hear and can therefore not listen to what is really being said.

3. Leaders should ask questions to draw information from the employees. But questions intended to test an employee's knowledge, although valuable in certain other situations, have no place in communication.

TIP: Effective questions are formed by asking what, where, how, and why. Listen with the intent of exploring the answer.

WHEN PREPARATION AND OPPORTUNITY MEET

Motivational factors must be challenging, achievable, and desirable. If the goals of the company and the goals of the employees do not coincide, the goals cannot be used as motivators.

1. To inspire others, you must be watchful of certain motivation killers. Assigning the most efficient employees the most difficult tasks, or giving them the heaviest workload simply because you know that the work will get done, will reward the slackers and punish the good workers.

2. Finding a person's talents requires a true interest in finding his or her talents. In other words, you must care about him more than you care about your title.

3. If you want to see an employee shine, you must place him or her in a position where he can use his talents. No talent becomes evident until preparation and opportunity meet. Having the opportunity to use the talent is at least as important as having the talent itself.

TIP: The employee is the ultimate judge of what position is right for him or her. The best you can do is question and guide.

WHICH WAY IS THE WHEEL TURNING?

Whether the wheel that squeaks gets the grease or whether silence is golden is a matter of timing. Whether a quiet person is a good or bad communicator is a matter of timing.

1. When we say that something is "everybody's responsibility," we diminish the value of the responsibility. When we say that a leader should be good at thirty different things, we likewise diminish the value of each of these things.

2. Before conducting a job interview with an applicant, find out how objective you are by asking yourself if the applicant's answers will really matter. If you knew nothing about him or her, would you hire or not hire him based solely on his answers?

3. Selecting a good candidate for the job takes a willingness to challenge assumptions, even those coming from superiors, experts, or "reliable sources."

TIP: When determining where somebody fits, you might want to start by looking at recurring patterns in his or her performance. Even qualities that initially seem undesirable, such as not working well with others, interrupting others in conversation, being impatient, or demanding that all work be finished an hour early, are not by nature bad qualities. They only become so when we misunderstand how to use them, or when we try to eradicate or change them instead of making good use of them. Ask, "Which way is the wheel turning?"

WHO WANTS A CHALLENGE?

It has been said that great leaders venture out and find challenges.

1. Keep in mind that the leader cannot exist without the followers and many followers are not interested in challenges that will upset their daily routine.

2. To convince an individual to agree with a conclusion, you must first convince him or her to agree with the premises. If he or she does not agree with the premises, the conclusion will never follow.

3. You can force change, but if you do your team will not respect you as a leader, they will not stand behind you. You will lose your most important asset: your people.

TIP: Don't implement change solely for the sake of seeking a challenge. Change can take many directions and a solution that works well for one company or leader may not work equally well for another under similar circumstances.

WINNING MATTERS

You must win to acquire a following. To retain leadership a leader must succeed more often than he loses.

1. But the leader's job is not to win at all cost, lest he might score a pyrrhic victory when the opposition rises up to smite him. Few people are willing to sacrifice their health, sleep, well-being, or family for their boss or company.

2. Although leadership is about character (or to extend the cliché: Leadership is to *have* character but not *be* a character), it is NOT about flattering yourself over your ability to think up clever slogans. And even character cannot win if the strategy is poor.

3. The team is not for everybody. As politically wrong as it sounds, the team must discriminate; it must include some people while excluding others. Pride comes from knowing that you are unique, stronger, and better than the competition. Teamwork is not about creating a win-win situation. Rather, the team is zero-sum: We win, you lose.

TIP: It matters less whose team you are on as long as you are on the winning team. We admire Napoleon Bonaparte, not because he had great character, but because he knew how to win.

WORLD'S GREATEST

Your vision statement tells you who you are and where you want to go. But it implies something *different* than what you presently are or have. To become different than what you are, you must first know what you are.

1. The vision, "to be the world's greatest," is weak because it fails to define who you are, who you need to defeat, and what you must do to reach your objective. In practical terms, it is as useful (or useless) as "to become a millionaire," or "to understand the meaning of life."

2. How do you define "greatest"? According to what criteria, and who is the judge? The world's greatest, how? In size? In service? In revenue? All of the above?

3. A vision should be like a wave to the surfer, with an uplifting and accelerating push from behind.

TIP: Being the greatest for the sake of being the greatest is meaningless. State the steps in order to create purpose. If you don't know the steps, you have no business stating the vision.

CONCLUSION

The purpose of leadership is not to improve the leader in the form of ego, money, convenience, or job security. The best leaders draw from the resourcefulness of their team and take the team beyond the leader's own level of skill. The leader is the assistant to the team, and is at the mercy of the team. He gives the team the benefit of the doubt while risking the mistakes and blunders. The best leaders are respected for their courage and honesty even when they are carriers of bad news.

Although it might appear as though a good team leader wears many hats (leader, friend, problem solver, and role model), he works primarily in a support role to the team. Good leadership requires maintenance. It is not enough to tell your team what you want them to do. You must also follow up, give feedback, and give each member an opportunity to voice his or her concerns. To have a positive and lasting impact on the members of your team, you must respect the fact that people are different. When you and your team meet in this way, you may feel invincible. This is what makes consistent victory possible. There is no greater feeling!

ABOUT THE AUTHOR

Martina Sprague has a Master of Arts Degree in Military History from Norwich University in Vermont. As a historian she is particularly interested in political and social factors that influence the decisions of "Great Men" and the actions of their subordinates. She has written numerous books about military and political/social history. For more information, please visit her Web site: www.modernfighter.com.

www.ingramcontent.com/pod-product-compliance
Lightning Source LLC
Chambersburg PA
CBHW061512180526
45171CB00001B/150